THE SHORT BOOK OF
being an
INVESTOR
not a
SPECULATOR

How to achieve a fair return from
investment markets

M.A. WYLIE

*With investing "you need to know
what you don't know".*

The Short Book of Being an Investor not a Speculator

© Mark Wylie 2018

Layout by Michael Hanrahan Publishing
Cover design by Peter Reardon

ISBN: 9780648402428

ABOUT THE BOOK

The Short Book of Being an Investor not a Speculator includes information on:

- Choosing which investments to buy and which to stay away from

- Including index managed funds ETF's, and cash product

- When to buy, hold and sell

- Minimising the fees and costs of investing

- Construction of a portfolio and maintaining it

- When to review investments

- Making a plan to invest that works for you

This book is an ideal resource for those new and existing investors favouring a fundamental approach to investment that will identify more stable investments that should deliver long-term market net returns. It is suitable for self-managed superannuation funds (SMSF's), investment funds etc.

The Short Book of Being an Investor not a Speculator is a practical guide that builds on Mark Wylie's first five books about long-term investing. The author shows how his methods can successfully be implemented by people who don't have much time or technical knowledge. Mark examines how to construct a wise long-term investment portfolio with a margin of safety, including index managed funds and or exchange traded funds (ETF's), bonds and cash alternatives.

ABOUT THE AUTHOR

Mark Wylie is a practical investor living in South Australia. Mark favours a fundamental and analytical approach to investment and has researched the great investors particularly Warren Buffett's methods. Mark holds a diploma of Financial Advising and launched his mentoring business in 2002. His aim is to help investors understand investing and in particular long-term investing, to help them develop strategies for themselves that would yield market or better returns.

Mark has authored five books on investing and experienced up-close the substantial world market corrections of the Global Financial Crisis (GFC) – the worst since the Great Depression – and now in this book he shares the knowledge and experience that he has gained over his 35+ years of working in the investment industry.

CONTENTS

Chapter 1

INTRODUCTION

I started my equity investment life when I was 30 years of age. I should have started earlier. However I did save and bought my first home when I was 21. A good start but not an ideal one! I could have done better with the right plan earlier in life.

Since I started investing I have endeavoured to research and understand what I was about to do, to not rush in without the proper background. Towards that end I have studied the great investors of the world to learn the messages they offer: Benjamin Graham, Warren Buffett and Charlie Munger to name a few. These three have been my idols in the investment arena. We all need a mentor or coach whether it's official or adopted as I have.

I have learned a lot over my investing career and the most profound thing I have discovered is to be like Benjamin Graham, Warren Buffett and Charlie Munger is extremely difficult as they are truly unique individuals with strong discipline to keep to their methodologies through good and bad times. Most investors will never achieve their returns. Accepting those men are unique and allowing yourself to find what works for you is far more important. This book will help you explore how to obtain your fair share of market returns over the long term.

Equity markets giveth and taketh but as investors we are seeking the net give over time; the net give is what companies generate over time as dividends and capital growth. Unfortunately, there are periods of time when the market does not value the earnings and growth particularly well, but reversion to the mean does occur in the long haul.

This is my sixth book on investing and I have focused my years of investing into this all-new edition. I hope it helps investors of any age. To be successful with investing we need to focus on the longer term. Markets go up and down regularly, we need to follow the trend which is generally upwards over the long term. Investing requires a longer than five year time frame otherwise you're a Speculator. I aim to help you, whether you are a new or existing investor, establishing your plan and methodology to see you finish life with enough money, however much that may be.

I hope you enjoy and find my book helpful. Happy investing.

Best wishes.

Mark

Chapter 2

GETTING YOUR LIFE IN ORDER TO INVEST FOR YOUR FUTURE

Before you commence investing it's important you get your finances in order, to let you invest. I suggest the following set of guidelines:

1. Pay off all your credit card debt as quickly as you can and always pay the due balance off each month. Not spending more than you have is very important to maintain financial control of your life.

2. Each pay day or when income is received you should save at least 10% and if you can 15-20%. Make automatic deductions each pay period.

3. Make maximum contributions to your superannuation. This can be part or all of the savings in item 2 above.

4. Never buy or sell individual company equity stocks unless you know what you are really doing! Even when you think you know what you're doing, do you really? With individual stock, "you really need to know what you don't know".

5. For most investors I suggest buying low-cost Managed Funds Indexes or Exchange Traded Funds (ETF's) index funds.

6. If you decide you need the extra assistance of a Financial Advisor make them commit to their fiduciary duty and standards to you the client. The fees paid to them should be transparent and at a fixed rate agreement.

7. Only when you are financially sound should you buy a residential home for yourself/family.

That's if you want to own property, you may choose not to, that's up to you.

8. A very important part of your financial plans is to have the right amount of insurances: life, income, trauma, business, property and contents etc… make sure you and your family are protected.

When you have the above list of important items and suggestions understood and under control then it's time to invest wisely for your future.

Remember be the Tortoise not the Hare in this marathon of life.

I will further expand upon the investing aspects above in later chapters.

Chapter 3

UNDERSTANDING COMPOUNDING GROWTH (INTEREST)

The definition of Compounding Interest is as follows according to the Australian Securities & Investment Commission (ASIC):

> *"Compounding interest is interest paid on the initial principle as well as the accumulated interest on money you have borrowed or invested. Compounding interest is like double chocolate topping on your savings. You earn interest on the money you deposit, and on the interest you have already earned – so you earn interest on interest. An online savings account paying monthly interest is an example of an account that earns compounding interest."*

> *"The Compounding Effect – If you invest $10,000 for 5 years at 5% per year, with interest paid at the end of the term, you would earn $2,500 in simple interest after 5 years, $500 for each year. This would give you a total of $12,500 after 5 years."*

> *"If you invested $10,000 for 5 years at 5% with interest calculated and added monthly, you would earn $2834 in compounding interest after 5 years, giving you a total of $12,834. Returns would be higher because you'd earned interest on your interest."*

To put this in the world of investing when you invest in companies they hopefully earn money and some of that is given to you as a dividend and some is reinvested back into the company to help it grow further. You can also reinvest your dividends back into that company or others to improve the results even more. Superannuation funds do this until you move into pension mode and that's why

Superannuation can be an excellent way to prepare for your retirement years.

**Figure 3.1 – Example of the results
from compounding interest**

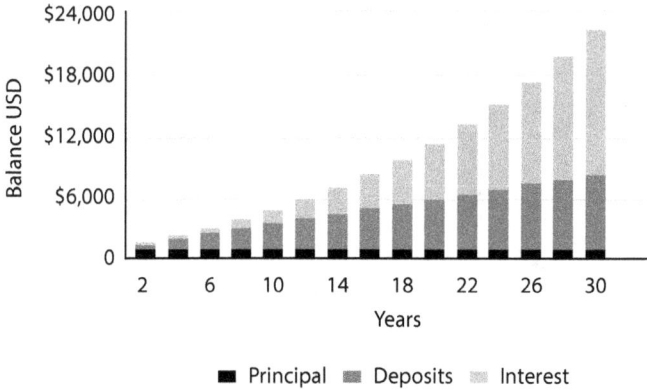

■ Principal ▓ Deposits ░ Interest

Chapter 4

BE AN
INVESTOR
NOT
SPECULATOR

INVESTMENT METHODOLOGY GUIDELINES

This is an introduction to how to take control of your finances to achieve independence and achieve your life goals.

1. *Develop a simple plan you understand* – your investment planning starts with some estimates of what kind of money you will need to meet your goals in the future. These can seem formidable, but nevertheless you need to establish them realistically and meaningfully.

2. *Start to invest early and make it automatic* – as we saw before, the miracle of compounding growth takes time so it's very important to start early in your life. If you are older then start now.

3. *Understand your investment risks* – it's important to have the right balance of stock and bonds/deposits for your age bracket. As you get older you need to lower your risk by moving more to bond/deposits for your security in retirement.

4. *Diversify, Diversify* – apart from owning stocks in diverse index funds you need to own bonds, deposits and cash.

5. *Don't ever try to time the market* – only a small percentage of investors will ever get timing the market right, I suggest you don't even try unless you really know what you are doing. Dollar cost averaging is a far better way to introduce money to the investment market. I will talk about this method later in the book.

6. *Invest in Index Funds, Mutual Funds and Exchange Traded Funds (ETF's)* – I will talk about these in later chapters.

7. *Keep all costs low* – costs are a killer when investing so find investments with high quality and low fees, like the range of Vanguard funds (I explain them later). The more you transact the more fees you pay so keep transactions to a minimum.

8. *Understand your taxes and keep them minimised* – use tax advantage methods like Superannuation to hold your investments. I suggest professional tax advice is very important. Get the right structure from the beginning.

9. *KISS, Keep It Simple Stupid* – keeping things simple will lead you to success, the more boring the investment process is will lead to the best results, you don't have to be The Wolf of Wall Street!

10. *Now you must stay the long term* – going along this path you will be tempted to change plans when times get rough but you need to go through the storm with great focus on the goals in sight. Short-term fluctuations are just that, short term, what you want is to stay with the long-term upward trending market. Keep reviewing your plan and stick to it.

Investors seek to find the true fundamentals of a business and invest in those businesses that meet a set of criteria which indicate a quality business. Speculators look for short-term profits from changes in a market price and generally have no interest in the company's business fundamentals. Speculators try to find mismatches in pricing of equities in the market and trade them for a profit. This type of trading tends to be a risky process which needs close attention all the time. Most private investors don't have the skills and the time to make it work for them, that's why I recommend being an investor and not a speculator most of the time. Figure 4.1 shows the returns of being a constant investor over the long term.

Figure 4.1 – The Dow Jones Industrial Average 1896 – 2016

All Ordinaries Accumulation Index adjusted for CPI inflation (2012 prices)

2000s mining and credit boom

1980s entrepreneurial boom then property boom

Late 1960s mining boom

1930s depression recovery

Late 1990s dot-com boom

Early 1970s property finance boom

War build-up boom

1950s consumer boom

1920s boom

Chapter 5

HAVING AN INVESTMENT PLAN THAT WORKS

If you don't have a plan you won't know where you are going to end up!

Having a workable plan is essential when investing, it does not need to be complex, it's actually better to have just a simple plan that you completely understand. Otherwise, you are going to get confused along the way.

An example plan is as follows:

1. Save 10% or more of my income and invest each month into a Superannuation Fund or Investment Fund Portfolio.

2. Invest for the long term and don't trade in the short term.

3. Invest in a balanced mix of Index Funds or Exchange Traded Funds (ETF's). Diversification is the aim here.

4. Invest in a mix of investments both domestically and internationally.

5. Keep investing monthly until you retire or need the money to live off.

6. Monitor your investment performance each quarter and perhaps rebalance if one or more of the funds have performed better than expected. The proceeds can be used to add to and rebalance your investments. I will have some examples later in the book.

7. Plan to keep invested during good and bad times and if you are able to invest more during a correction that would be advantageous.

Remember:

"Be fearful when others are greedy and greedy when others are fearful" – *Warren Buffett*

8. Keep fees and costs to an absolute minimum. This is one of the most important things to do when investing wisely.

The list above should help you generate a workable plan. Your plan must suit your needs and situation, everybody's will be different. Once you have a plan review it at least once or twice a year and adjust it as and when you feel it is needed. Plans need to be flexible and change to meet current times; being adaptable is important to being a wise investor.

Chapter 6

HOW TO
INVEST
WISELY

To invest wisely for most people means taking a long-term approach to their investing methodology. It's not about trying to be the 'Wolf of Wall Street', only a very few investors can achieve that style and ability of investment! For most of us we should be the Tortoise and not the Hare.

To achieve the 'investing wise' way we need a plan as I discussed in the last chapter. Work with this plan over the long term without losing focus along the journey. The journey will be filled with events that test us mentally and financially. If we watch the market daily we may well get frustrated with the seemingly stupid way the market reacts. The market giveth and taketh away, it's the net giveth that is what we are looking for over the long term.

Short-term investing will generate less than market returns because of all the transaction costs and taxes involved. Many traders kid themselves about what their real returns are. As Rene Rivkin once said "I never met a wealthy chartist". People like Warren Buffett, who is one of the wealthiest investors in the world, have built their wealth over a lifetime and in his case since he was a young child. Now in his 80's he is reaping the rewards of his patience. Berkshire Hathaway's Deputy Chairman Charlie Munger says "money flows from the impatient to the patient".

It's not rocket science, it's about putting away each week, month, quarter as much of your income as you can afford, hopefully 10%+ if you can. Make it an automatic deduction once you get paid, then you can spend what is left over.

Investment tips from your mate, taxi driver or who-ever, hardly ever turn out well. If it sounds too good to be true then it normally is! Alway invest with proper invest-ment companies like Vanguard Investments (see in later chapter), making sure they are reputable and provide proper credentials. When investing you must also receive proper paperwork, not just a false promise to return your money one day. Friends and family can be the worst people to invest with! When you invest your hard-earned money it must be in business-like transactions which have been researched properly for true investment crite-ria. Basically don't trust anyone with your money unless they are truly legitimate.

Business perspective investing is a term which is used to describe an approach to investing that is fully researched and without any emotional feeling being involved in the selection process. If after rigorous testing of sound business criteria the investment is strong then once the purchase price is acceptable and with a mar-gin of safety evident, a purchase could be made for your portfolio with solid evidence.

Margin of safety is also a common term and means buying below an investment's Intrinsic Value so to allow for any error in your price assessment. In Appendix A, I describe how to calculate intrinsic value. If you think about this like going to a shopping centre and finding that one of your favourite purchases is on sale at half price, it's a bargain!

Chapter 7

WHICH INVESTMENTS TO BUY

As suggested before, a mixture of Index Fund type investments should do the job for you. But before we talk about which investments let's look at some life strategy asset allocations.

Figure 7.1 – Life Strategy Asset Allocation Chart

TEENS TO THIRTIES (The "Getting Started" Years)

Situation & Goals
*Aggressive
*Growing net worth
*Very long-term outlook
*Willing to take a fair amount of risk

Aggressive Growth	5% To 10%	5%
Growth	40% To 50%	45%
Growth & Income	30% To 40%	35%
Term Deposit	5% To 15%	10%
Cash	5% To 10%	5%
Total		100%

◦ Aggressive Growth	5% To 10%
◦ Growth	40% To 50%
◦ Growth & Income	30% To 40%
◦ Term Deposit	5% To 15%
◦ Cash	5% To 10%

THIRTIES TO FIFTIES 9 (The "Making Money" Years)

Situation & Goals
*Ten or more years to retirement
*Building net worth
*Willing to take risk
*Not needing investment income

Aggressive Growth	5% To 10%	5%
Growth	25% To 35%	35%
Growth & Income	35% To 45%	40%
Term Deposit	15% To 30%	15%
Cash	5% To 10%	5%
Total		100%

◦ Aggressive Growth	5% To 10%
◦ Growth	25% To 35%
◦ Growth & Income	35% To 45%
◦ Term Deposit	15% To 30%
◦ Cash	5% To 10%

FIFITY TO MID-SIXTIES (The "Preretirement" Years)

Situation & Goals
*Less than ten years to retirement
*Typically higher-income years with fewer financial issues
*Willing to take some risk but wanting less volatility

Aggressive Growth	0% To 5%	5%
Growth	15% To 25%	25%
Growth & Income	30% To 40%	40%
Term Deposit	20% To 30%	20%
Cash	5% To 10%	10%
Total		100%

◦ Aggressive Growth	0% To 5%
◦ Growth	15% To 25%
◦ Growth & Income	30% To 40%
◦ Term Deposit	20% To 30%
◦ Cash	5% To 10%

SIXTIES AND UP (The "Retirement" Years)

Situation & Goals
*Enjoying retirement or very close to retire
*Potecting net worth
*Preferring less risk

Aggressive Growth	0% To 5%	5%
Growth	10% To 20%	20%
Growth & Income	30% To 40%	35%
Term Deposit	25% To 35%	25%
Cash	10% To 15%	15%
Total		100%

◦ Aggressive Growth	0% To 5%
◦ Growth	10% To 20%
◦ Growth & Income	30% To 40%
◦ Term Deposit	25% To 35%
◦ Cash	10% To 15%

These are suggestions which should help guide you at the various stages of your life. In the following graph I suggest an index mix for Australian investors; if you are overseas you might prefer to swap the Australian index portion for your local one.

Figure 7.2 – Market Index Asset Mix Suggestion

ASSET TYPE	% ASSET MIX
Australian Share Index	30
USA Share Index	20
USA Moat Company Index	10
World Share Index Ex USA	30
Cash Or Equivalents	10

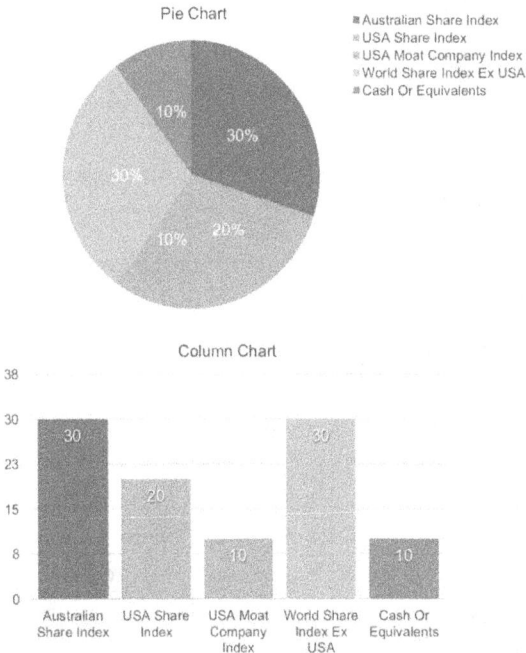

Pie Chart

- Australian Share Index
- USA Share Index
- USA Moat Company Index
- World Share Index Ex USA
- Cash Or Equivalents

Column Chart

Now let's discuss the sort of specific investments you could invest in. This is where Vanguard Investments can make life easier. Jack Bogle the founder of Vanguard Investments understood that for most investors they would do well to just invest in a fund that replicated the market indices. Bogle set out to build a business of creating Index Funds and more recently Exchange Traded Funds (ETF's) and now that business is the largest in the world for Index Fund investment products. There are others such as BlackRock, BetaShares and State Street Global, UBS, VanEck and Russell Investments.

For Australian Investors I offer suggestions purely by way of example below:

- Vanguard Australian Shares Index – ASX Code VAS

- Vanguard FTSE All World ex US – ASX Code VEU

- Vanguard U.S. Total Share Market Shares Index – ASX Code VTS

- Van Eck Vectors Morningstar Wide Moat – ASX Code Moat

- Cash – like a Cash Management Fund or Deposit Fund, somewhere you can get quick access for investing more during down times.

There are lots of listed index funds/ETF's now available and these are just a few; look around for ones that would suit your plan. Most world markets are covered by index funds these days also market sectors like emerging markets etc…

You might want to follow a particular index because you know that market and or industry.

For further details I suggest you visit Vanguard Investments's website, where there are many useful investment tools and resources to help you invest:

- Vanguard Investments USA – www.vanguard.com

- Vanguard Investments Australia – www.vanguard.com.au

Chapter 8

PLAN FOR
YOUR
RETIREMENT

Most governments around the world do not provide proper retirement benefits, so this means we all have to take control and plan for when we retire, especially if we want to live out our later years comfortably.

So as I have discussed earlier in this book we need to plan early and start saving for our retirement. In Australia all workers have some of their wages automatically placed into industry superannuation funds. This is a good start for most people however the percentage of wages needs to be increased to between 10% and 12% to ensure there will be enough to retire on comfortably. If you can put away more than 12% even better – again this should be automatically deducted each pay period.

Some people who have higher incomes might like to set up their own Self Managed Superannuation Fund (SMSF) which gives them more control over the investment chosen. The important issue here is to keep costs low as they eat into returns quickly. They also require a lot of compliance so they must be professionally managed. Generally SMSF's are only used if there are multiple members and investable funds of over $500,000 but there are some low-cost single SMSF platforms for individuals with smaller amounts.

A lack of planning for your retirement years can be devastating especially if you are forced to retire earlier than you planned. The pressures on spending your money in your earlier years is great, but don't bow to that pressure, keep your plan of saving for the future intact.

If you have an idea of how much you want in retirement then perhaps visit a financial advisor to help you plan to reach that goal.

Some financial advisors talk about spending no more than 4% of your superannuation capital amount per year. Once you decide on how much you need per year to live on then some calculations can be made. Below I have done a rough example for you:

This example is if you wanted $50,000 in retirement benefits per year.

$1,250,000 @ 4% P/A =$50,000
(you would need this amount in capital investments)

Now the trick here is to earn more than 4%+ per year and hopefully 7% or more. This way you should never run out of money.

If you wanted $100,000 in retirement benefits then you would need $2,500,000 in capital investments etc.

Chapter 9

HOW TO STRUCTURE YOUR INVESTMENT OWNERSHIP

Structuring investment ownership is a question for your Tax Accountant, as it requires expert advice to ensure you are protected and in the best tax environment. Please seek professional tax advice.

My comments here are only to make you think about your structure before you start investing. Making mistakes can be costly and we are all about keeping costs to a minimum.

The two main issues are asset protection and the best tax environment.

Most people will choose to hold investments within their Superannuation which generally offers asset protection and an excellent tax environment. If you decide to hold investments outside your Superannuation then this can be more complicated and needs careful thought.

The options are:

1. In your own name: this provides little asset protection and is not very tax effective.

2. In a company structure: this may offer some asset protection but won't offer much tax effectiveness.

3. In a Family Trust: this may offer improved asset protection and should offer better tax effectiveness but still won't be as good as Superannuation.

Clearly Superannuation is the best on offer but may not suit your situation so this is why you should seek professional advice about your structure.

These above structures can be costly to set up and maintain. Again your accountant should be able to advise on start-up costs and the yearly compliance costs. Superannuation might be the most cost effective way to invest which is why you need to fully understand all the options available.

If you don't have an accountant I suggest you find a reputable one to coach you through these tricky bits and help you maintain compliance during your investing life.

Chapter 10

MAKING
IT HAPPEN
AND
WORK

Once you have decided on a Structure and your account-ant has helped you get that in place, you are almost ready to invest.

Getting started is always hard, so as I said earlier just start saving money either into your Superannuation account or a Cash Management Trust (CMT) that can be linked to an online broker service like Macquarie Bank in Australia. Once you have built up say $1000 then buy an index fund ETF online. Don't forget it's got to be in keeping with your plan. Then keep buying when you get enough money in your CMT account; just make sure your buying fees/costs aren't too high to make it not feasible. Discount broker fees help here.

By investing when you have generated enough money to invest, say every three months or monthly if you earn more, you are actually doing what is called "Dollar Cost Averaging". This is a good way to invest as it averages your investment into the market. When times are good you end up buying fewer shares but when the time are bad you buy more shares, which means you average into the market over time. Now don't forget if the markets are way off their peaks then consider buying more shares, as long as the spare cash allows.

At this point I wish to say I do not support borrow-ing money to buy shares unless you are a well seasoned investor who knows exactly what are doing and understand all the down-side risks of margin lending. You have to completely understand what you are doing if you ever margin lend. It's for professionals not regular investors.

As I suggested in a previous chapter Vanguard Investments have an impressive set of resources and products that can be simply adopted to invest with and reduce your workload. Explore their websites. You might like to just invest using their managed funds. However there are minimum initial investment levels of $5000 AUD (Retail Client) for each fund you invest in, and $100 AUD from then if done by direct debit transfers.

Once you have the plan working don't forget to review your investment progress on a regular basis; when is up to you: weekly, monthly or quarterly as long as you do it. These reviews are important as things do change and sometimes quite quickly.

Chapter 11

FEES,
COSTS
AND
TAXATION

"But while the investors who trade the least have a fighting chance of capturing the market's return, those who trade the most are doomed to failure."
— John C. Bogle, founder of The Vanguard Group

Almost as important as thinking about how you are going to increase your investments is considering how you are going to minimise fees, taxation and other costs. A dollar saved is a dollar earned — that's true in the world of investment. If one dollar goes out of your account, that's one dollar less that you have available for making profits. However, if you structure your investments so that fees, taxation and other costs are minimised, you will be maximising your profit potential. And the longer you invest for, the bigger effect this will be.

FEES

Fees are an enemy to investors and need to be very well understood because they can erode an investor's return considerably over time. Even a small percentage over time can significantly change the investment outcome, as shown in Figure 11.1.

The negative compounding effect of fees is quite evident in the lower returns.

We will now have a look at the different types of fees charged for different investments. This will help you to make informed decisions about what fees you should be paying and, more importantly, those that you shouldn't be paying.

Figure 11.1 – Effect of Higher Costs over 10 Years

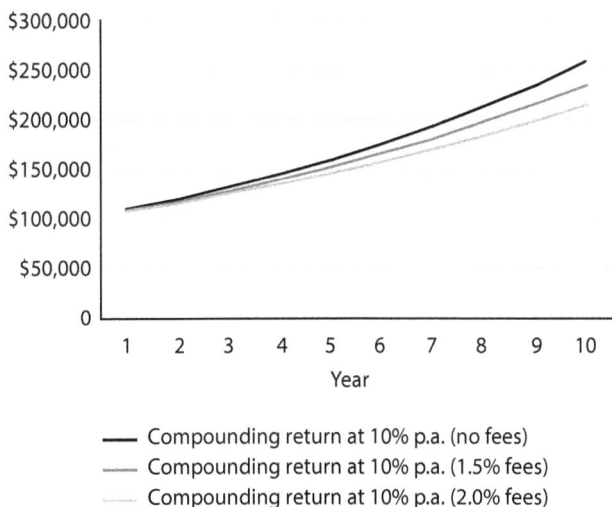

— Compounding return at 10% p.a. (no fees)
— Compounding return at 10% p.a. (1.5% fees)
— Compounding return at 10% p.a. (2.0% fees)

FUND MANAGER FEES AND COSTS

Management fees and costs for managed funds (such as index funds) can vary greatly from provider to provider and you need to understand the effects on your investment. These days, providers charge all sorts of fees; I do recommend when investing that you explore these fees and fully understand their effects before you invest. By law, funds must disclose all their fees in the product disclosure statement in a prescribed format, so read this carefully before you buy.

Some managers charge performance fees above a benchmark performance level. For example, a manager might charge 1% extra if the All Ordinaries Index is outperformed by 10%. These charges can be excessive. Excellent managers justify reasonable performance fees, but check out the fund you are buying into to make sure that managers are not rewarded for only average performance. You shouldn't be paying extra for beating an index by just 1% or 2%. Warren Buffett, the world's greatest fund manager, is paid about USD$200,000 per year and manages over USD$100 billion of investments – and receives no performance fees! (He still eats his own cooking!)

Some fees can be hidden, especially "entry" and "exit" fees. These can be paid to salespeople and managers. While you don't pay them directly, these costs will eventually be taken out of your returns somewhere along the line. These can be as high as 5% going in and out. All fees eventually detract from investment returns.

The costs that you might be charged by a managed fund include:

- *Entry or establishment fees* – this is a fee to open your account. This can be up to 5%.

- *Management fees* – these are the ongoing costs of running the fund.

- *Transaction costs* – these are expenses incurred by the fund in buying and selling investments.

- *Contribution fee* – this is charged every time you add to your investment. (This may not be possible with some funds.)

- *Switching fee* – you may be charged to switch from one investment to another within the one company.

- *Exit fee* – this is charged when you close your account. There may be a higher fee if you close your account within a specified period.

What level of fees do I consider fair and reasonable? The following are as a percentage of funds invested per annum.

High	1.00%+	Unreasonable
↑	1.00%	Acceptable just
│	0.75%	Fair and ok
┼	0.50%	Fair and reasonable
│	0.40%	Very fair and reasonable
↓		
Low	0.25%	Fantastic

I also think this should include all administration and accounting fees.

So far I have talked about the more obvious fees, however when you buy and sell some broker fees will occur. Most large fund managers would negotiate low fees for brokerage, but still even a small fee, say 0.3% in and out, adds up and reduces investor returns. The more transactions the smaller investor returns.

BROKERAGE

Brokerage is of course the fee you pay to your stockbroker for executing a buy or sell order for you. You might also choose to pay for investment advice.

A discount broker is one that just executes orders for you, and offers no advice. Most of them operate over the internet these days, and are therefore known as "internet brokers". They often have company research and information on their website. The fees for an internet broker will be lower than for a full-service broker. Such brokers might charge a fixed fee of, say, $30 per transaction for orders under $10,000, and then brokerage will usually be negotiable over $10,000. Many banks and other financial institutions offer such a service these days. They are usually quite similar, so shop around for one that offers the services you require with the lowest fees. Don't pay for any extras that you have no use for. Some also offer facilities to make trades over the phone, though this is usually slightly more expensive. Keep in mind that some brokers advertise low rates that only apply to certain customers, such as those who make a minimum number of trades per month.

A full-service broker is one that provides ... full service! As well as executing your orders, they will meet with you to discuss your investment goals and your financial circumstances, and will also provide advice on which shares they think you should buy given your investment style and current market conditions. A full-service broker can also offer ongoing portfolio management, and may provide access to restricted company floats that you might not otherwise have.

As a small investor you will be doing your own research, but it's never a bad thing to get another opinion and discuss your options. Just make sure that you still understand the decisions that are being made. If you choose full service, listen to your broker but don't let them run the show.

Of course, a full-service broker will have higher fees. You might pay $100 or $150 per transaction, and you could pay an hourly fee for meetings and advice. Find out exactly what the fees include, and make sure you are only paying for services that you need. Brokerage may be negotiable with a full-service broker if you have a large account. Give it a try – they can only say no!

BANK FEES

You will of course pay fees to operate bank accounts. Make sure you understand what is and what is not included with an account, and don't pay for any features you don't need. For example, don't pay extra for a cheque account if you do all of your banking over the internet. There are many different types of financial institutions out there, so shop around.

TAXATION

The costs associated with buying and selling regularly reduce investor returns, through both fees and taxation. Every time a "sell" is made, if a profit is achieved then taxation on this transaction is applicable. Some managers turn over their portfolios 100% or more per year. This excessive amount of transactions erodes the compounding effect of funds invested over time. The money you pay in taxes you cannot earn more investment returns on – it's a lost opportunity.

If you do want to place some of your money in a fund, some types of funds are better than others. A significant advantage of index funds is that they don't buy and sell excessively, which helps to keep taxation down for investors. An index fund manager will only buy and sell in an effort to match the construction of an index, and will not trade in an attempt to find the best shares and higher returns. Excessive trading often actually decreases profits, both from the return on shares and also increased fees and taxes. (Table 11.1 shows the taxation effects of different levels of turnover.) Also, don't forget that not all trades will be profitable, and then a loss of capital can occur and that also reduces returns and funds invested.

Table 11.1 – The Tax Cost of High Portfolio Turnover

Real after-tax returns: Wholesale	Turnover impact on average fund			
	Vanguard®	Low efficiency	Medium efficiency	High efficiency
Investment amount 1 July 2006	$500,000	$500,000	$500,000	$500,000
Total return %	28.8%	26.8%	26.8%	26.8%
Growth return %	22.6%	5.4%	5.4%	5.4%
Income return %	6.2%	21.4%	21.4%	21.4%
Growth on investment amount	$113,000	$27,064	$27,064	$27,064
Income earned on investment amount	$30,900	$107,182	$107,182	$107,182
Income tax payable	$11,891	$49,081	$39,098	$29,115
After-tax value of investment 30 June 2007	$632,009	$585,165	$595,148	$605,131
After-tax return year ended 30 June 2007	**26.4%**	**17.0%**	**19.0%**	**21.0%**
		9.4%	7.4%	5.4%

Source: Vanguard Investments

Taxation benefits should be considered a bonus. Yes, you should do your homework and attempt to legally minimise your tax obligations as much as possible, but an investment should never be made purely with tax benefits in mind. Any tax benefit gained will not make up for the bad performance of a poorly chosen investment.

Let's have a look at some ways that you can reduce the amount of tax you pay. But before we do, a word of warning: make sure you consult your accountant about all tax issues. It is perfectly legal for you to attempt to minimise your taxation obligation. However, there are some things that you can do that are illegal; for example, not reporting profits, attempting to hide money with complicated financial structures or making fraudulent transactions. You must get professional advice about whether a strategy that you are employing is legal. An investment transaction or structure will probably be questionable if it is made predominantly with the aim of avoiding tax. Severe penalties can apply for attempting to deceive the Tax Office.

CLAIMING DEDUCTIONS

Let's start with the easy one. Make sure you claim all tax deductions that you are entitled to. The Australian Taxation Office website (http://www.ato.gov.au) has information on what you can claim, or you can give them a call.

You might be able to claim:

- investment magazines and books that you purchase to help with your investments
- computer software related to your investing

- some fees, including bank fees on an investment account

- accounting fees relating to advice about your investments.

FRANKED DIVIDENDS

Many companies in Australia pay "fully franked dividends". This means that the dividend is paid out of the company's profits on which tax has already been paid. Investors who receive fully franked dividends will receive a tax credit that will reduce their own personal tax liability, because the money they are receiving has already had tax paid on it by the company. Some companies pay shares that are partly franked, meaning a partial tax credit will be received.

It's easy to find out if a company pays franked dividends. Simply look at its most recent annual report, or you can have a look at the share price tables in the daily newspaper.

Franked dividends can factor into your investment decisions, but they shouldn't be a priority. Never make an investment purely to receive franking credits. Any gain you might get from this will be lost – and then some –if the investment underperforms because it didn't meet your other criteria and you only bought it for the franking credits. But if you have two investments that both meet your criteria and one offers franking and the other doesn't, it could be beneficial to choose the company offering the credits.

INVESTING FOR MORE THAN 12 MONTHS

Investments held for more than 12 months can qualify for a 50% capital gains tax discount. As a small passive investor you will be aiming to hold for longer than this anyway, but this is something you should be aware of. (Talk to your accountant or tax adviser to find out what is most suitable for your situation.)

TIMING

Your timing for buying and selling an investment could affect when you pay tax on it, and possibly how much. This is especially true if you are considering buying or selling around 30 June (the end of the financial year) –talk to your accountant to see if you can vary the timing of the sale to improve your tax outcome, particularly if there are tax cuts looming.

SUMMARY

As you can see, a well-managed portfolio of good investments held for the long term should reduce your costs and improve returns. I believe a steady, long-term approach to holding investments is best, and it has the added advantage of reducing taxation and fees incurred by the investor, which in the long run will add significantly to returns. Never make an investment decision solely to reduce fees or tax, but always keep them in mind.

It is critically important that you talk to your accountant about these issues. Taxation is complicated, and there can be dire consequences if you undertake illegal activities in an attempt to reduce or avoid tax, even if you do so inadvertently. Always seek professional advice on such matters.

For more information, the Australian Taxation Office and the Australian Securities & Investments Commission both have very informative websites. Go to:

- http://www.ato.gov.au

- http://www.asic.gov.au

- http://www.moneysmart.gov.au
  (this is ASIC's website of financial and safety tips).

Chapter 12

CONTROLLING
YOUR
EMOTIONS

The psychology of investing is one of the most important aspects you need to master if you are to be a successful investor.

If you don't or can't control your emotions then you are going to go on an emotional roller coaster ride that may not end up well! The successful investors stay cool, calm and collected during all market cycles. They know what they are looking for as per their plan and will act when the timing is right for them and not be forced by others to act. Wise investors tend to be contrarian and do the opposite to the crowd. They buy when things are down and sell or hold when things are high. They just don't let emotions take over and panic. They understand the market whims and work it to suit themselves and not others.

Investing must be businesslike and not emotional, it must be based on true facts and not false hopes and wishes. The true past of a business must be understood to make any reasonable assessment of its future. Buying a business on shallow forecasts and unproved concepts can be very risky unless you have a full understanding of that business. Stick to ones with proven histories of performance.

Market ups and downs can be quick and unannounced and wise investors are always ready for what happens next because they expect something to happen even though they won't know what and when. As Warren Buffett states, you have to be prepared, as markets can drop 50% or more sometimes and if you can't stomach that then don't invest in equity markets.

I can't emphasise enough that this issue can effect your ability to be a sound investor. Work out prior to investing what your emotional tendencies are, and if you can't control yourself seek advice – it may save you a lot of stress and money.

Also talk to a financial advisor if you don't think you can cope with the emotional side of investing.

It may also be helpful to read some books on the subject of the psychology of investing.

Chapter 13

CONCLUSION

"Only buy something that you'd be perfectly happy to hold if the market shut down for 10 years." – Warren Buffett

This style of investing is an approach that will not suit all investors. It involves research, investigation and patience. It is not fancy, and it's not fast-paced. Long-term investing requires a plan, discipline, patience, time and a methodical manner. Without these qualities you might find it difficult and frustrating. If you are interested in investing because it seems exciting or you think it's a good way to make a quick dollar, this approach is not for you – and you are destined for failure in the investment market.

Warren Buffett and his Berkshire Hathaway company have demonstrated that, over time, careful long-term investing can pay great returns. It is a simple approach that can be used by the average investor. It doesn't require large capital resources, insider business knowledge or a fancy computer system. Once your portfolio is established, you do not need to monitor it on a day-to-day basis, so it's ideal for those who want to invest in their spare time.

It can take time to perform the investment analysis on a number of investments, but if you are patient and stick to the plan your hard work will be well rewarded. You will come away with a solid long-term portfolio, and possibly some stellar performers that will add substantially to your wealth.

Always remember the central themes of "Being An Investor Not a Speculator":

1. Conduct your research thoroughly, and only buy those investments that meet your investment criteria.

2. Perform the investigations yourself and make your own decisions.

3. Always leave a margin of safety between the investment price and the intrinsic value.

4. Ensure that your portfolio is diversified and well balanced.

5. Be aware of what the markets and the economy are doing, and re-visit your investments if you see reason to.

6. Always stick to the plan.

This style of investing can be started any time, even with small amounts of money. You might like to help your children start a small portfolio once they are old enough to have an interest. Take advantage of the power of compounding interest, and start your children investing at an early age.

For most people, trading shares is too difficult, or they don't have the skills or time to undertake the process properly. This book has looked at some other options to give you an understanding of long-term investing, so that if you don't do it all yourself you still have the knowledge to select somebody to undertake the investing for you, such as an investment adviser, a fund manager, a large investment institution or a listed investment company.

It's up to you now. Remember that your decisions are only as good as your research. Pay attention to what is going on in the markets. Conduct your reviews thoroughly. Read the financial news and follow your investments. Always be on the lookout for new opportunities, and always stick to your system – don't let greed or fear sway your decisions. This book has presented a method and process for you to follow that will greatly assist your investment performance. I hope I have shown you an alternative to short-term investing or trading that suits your style.

Good luck with your investing.

Appendix A

CALCULATING INTRINSIC VALUE

CALCULATING INTRINSIC VALUE

Calculating intrinsic value can be a complicated process, and you must have good mathematical skills to do so. You can create your own spreadsheet that will work it out for you (as I have done), or you can purchase some existing software. I only suggest working it out yourself if you understand the calculation and have the necessary skills. If not, you can use the available calculators as discussed in Chapter 4 of my book *The Sensible Australian Investor*.

DISCOUNTED CASH FLOW

Before performing the intrinsic value calculation, you must understand discounted cash flow. This is because the intrinsic value calculation is a method of discounting the future earnings of the share back to the present; if you do not understand the concept of discounted cash flow, the intrinsic value of a share will also make little sense. So, let's have a look.

What is a discounted cash flow?

A discounted cash flow (often known as a DCF) is a calculation performed to establish the value of money in the future, based on a set of assumptions. It can be used to establish the value of an investment by analysing expected future cash flows for the business. The expected returns to the investor are then discounted to arrive at a present-day value for the share. If the discounted value is greater than the current price of the share, it may be a buying opportunity. Confused? It's not really that difficult, it can just sound a bit daunting when encountered for the first time.

Businesses use this type of calculation all the time to make decisions about large amounts of capital; whether to purchase an expensive new computer system, for example, or whether to sell a piece of land that is not being used. For a new computer system, the amount of money saved over the next, say, five years by using a more efficient and reliable system would be weighed against the cost of purchasing the equipment today. And if selling a block of land, a business would examine trends in the property market to see if the return from the sale would be better now or in, say, two years' time. These could become very complicated calculations: the business looking at the computer system would need to factor in items such as staff salaries to see how much money would be saved from a faster system, possible down time for the installation of the new system and staff training. The seller of a property would need to factor in the costs of holding the land and the costs of selling. But no matter how complicated these equations become, the aim is always to answer a simple question: how much will an item or amount of money be worth at a given time in the future, based on all relevant income and costs? It converts a future amount to today's money.

HOW DOES DCF WORK?

Let's have a look at a very basic DCF example to demonstrate the concept: what would you do if somebody offered to give you $20,000 now or $20,000 in five years' time? You would of course take the $20,000 now. You do not need to perform any calculations to see why this is a better choice. If you invested the $20,000 now, or even just put it in the bank, you could have quite a bit more than $20,000 in five years' time. And even if you wanted to spend the money, you could buy more now with the same amount than you could later, because inflation will erode the value of the money.

But what if you were offered $20,000 now or $30,000 in five years' time? How do you know which is better? To make this decision, you need to work out what the $20,000 will be worth in five years. If you are a good investor, could you turn $20,000 into more than $30,000 in this time? What if you would take the money now and just put it in the bank? Will it be worth more than $30,000 in five years' time?

To work out what a given amount today will be worth in the future is a discounted cash flow calculation. To perform this calculation, you must know what return you expect to achieve and what period of time you are examining. In our example, the period of time is five years, and – to demonstrate how the DCF calculation is useful – we will assume two different levels of returns: 4% and 10%.

If you are a good investor who can achieve 10% annual returns, in five years' time your $20,000 will be worth $32,210. But if you are just going to stick it in the bank at 4%, in five years it will only be worth $24,333.

You can see how useful this type of calculation is: if you think you can achieve a 10% annual return you would take the $20,000 now, because in five years you will have $32,210; if you would just put it in the bank at 4%, you would obviously be better off waiting five years and taking the $30,000. If you did not know how to use discounted cash flow, how could you make this choice? Unfortunately, this is not a decision I've ever had to make, but I would know how to work it out if it ever comes up!

To keep this example simple, I have ignored inflation and costs, but these can also be factored into the figures. Inflation and costs will of course affect both outcomes.

Using a calculator for DCF

A discounted cash flow calculation is quite simple once you understand it and have the right calculator. I use a Texas Instruments BA 11 Plus calculator to perform all my discounted cash flow calculations, but any decent financial calculator will be able to perform this operation.

To perform the calculation, you need three of the following four pieces of information:

1. The interest rate or rate of return, represented by the symbol I/Y. Let's use our 4% we would receive from the bank.

2. The number of periods or years, represented by the symbol N. We have been using five, for five years.

3. The present value, represented by the symbol PV. We want to see what the $20,000 will be worth in five years, so our PV is 20,000.

4. The future value, represented by the symbol FV. Our FV will be the outcome of the calculation; that is, what the $20,000 will be worth in five years.

So our figures would look like this:

> *Interest rate: 4%*
> *Present value (enter as negative): −$20,000*
> *Number of years (periods): 5*
> *Future value (outcome of the calculation): $24,333*

This is how I would perform this calculation on my Texas Instruments calculator (most financial calculators will be similar):

1. Enter "4", then press the "I/Y" button.

2. Enter "20,000" and +/− to get negative, then press the "PV" button.

3. Enter "5", then press the "N" button.

4. Press the CPT button.

5. Press the FV button.

6. The answer of 24,333 will appear on the screen.

You can enter this information in any sequence; it will not matter.

You can use any three variables to find the fourth. For example, by entering the present value, the future value and the time period, you can find the return required to reach this future value. Or by entering the present value, the future value and the return, you can find out how long it will take to reach this future value. Or you can even start with the return, the future value and the period, and calculate what present value will give you this outcome (remember this: it will come in handy for intrinsic value).

You can also use this method to understand the effect of inflation on the value of money. For example, if inflation is 2.5%, you can perform the above calculation with a return figure of −2.5%; the minus is used because inflation is causing the value of your money to decrease by 2.5%, not increase as with the bank interest used above.

Once you understand DCF you will appreciate the process of intrinsic valuation, because it involves the same concept of discounting future value back to a present value. Using the terms and four input variables described above to find the intrinsic value we use the anticipated returns (equivalent to the interest rate) to establish the expected future return to the shareholder (the future value) over a given number of years (periods). What's the final of the four variables? The present value. An intrinsic value calculation will calculate the present value for us; that is, the current share price that fairly reflects the expected future returns. If the current actual share price is below the calculated intrinsic value of the share, this could be an opportunity to buy. If the current actual share price is above the calculated intrinsic value, then the share is not worthy of consideration, as the amount paid for the share now does not reflect how much money will be returned to the shareholder in the future.

Is this all making sense? Don't worry if you are finding these concepts difficult to grasp at first; just read back over the explanations. They will make sense once you have read through them a few times.

ESTABLISHING INTRINSIC VALUE

You should obtain financial data on the review company that includes up to 10 years of historical information. If you cannot find 10 years, just find as much detail as you can, but remember that the more historical data you have the more accurate your analysis will be.

Before you begin, make sure you have the following figures handy for as many years as possible:

- the number of shares on issue
- earnings per share
- depreciation or depreciation per share
- total capital expenditure or capital expenditure per share
- dividends per share, including any special dividends
- shareholder equity (also known as book value)
- price/earnings ratios
- your forecast percentage return (make sure you include inflation in this figure; if your forecast return is 10% and you expect inflation to be 2%, then your forecast return should actually be 12%)
- net tangible assets or net tangible assets per share
- your estimated future 10-year average price/ earnings ratio
- the current share price.

Different tools will require slightly different information to perform the calculation; if you have gathered the data above, you should be able to use such software to work out the intrinsic value of a company you are interested in.

Appendix B

8 STEPS TO WISE INVESTING

8 STEPS TO WISE INVESTING

Step 1. Read and learn about investment – lots of books just like this one.

Step 2. Decide when to start investing – now, or as soon as you can.

Step 3. Decide how much and how often – you need $1,000+ to start.

Step 4. Decide what type of investor you are:

- Active, which is time consuming and stressful.

- Passive, which requires limited time and is less stressful.

Step 5. Decide how to invest:

- Directly, active: selection of companies to invest into.

- Indirectly, diversified: selection of index investments.

Step 6. Decide what to invest into: which investment types suit you and your portfolio.

Step 7. Decide when to buy, hold and sell.

Step 8. Decide when to retire in advance and move to cash deposits and other safer investments (preferably before a market crash).

SUMMARY

The "four quadrant investor": which one are you?

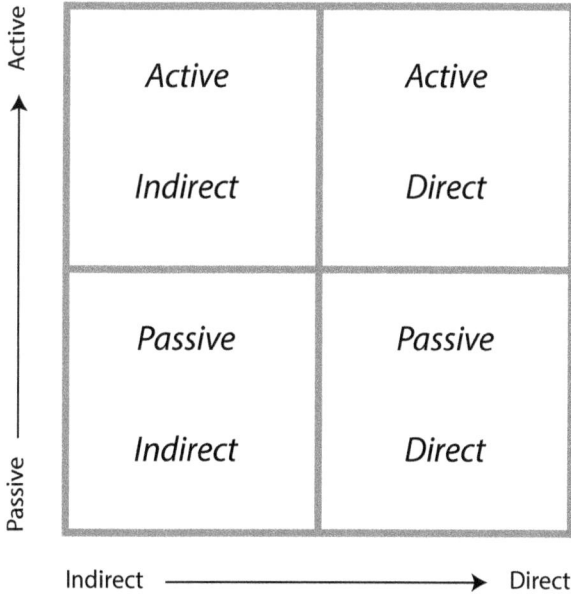

Active *Indirect*	*Active* *Direct*
Passive *Indirect*	*Passive* *Direct*

Active ↑   Passive (vertical axis, bottom to top)

Indirect ——————→ Direct (horizontal axis)

INVESTMENT GLOSSARY

All Ordinaries Index – The index that represents around 500 of Australia's largest companies. It is often used as a measure of the overall performance of the Australian market.

asset allocation – The proportion of your money that is invested in each of a range of assets.

Australian Securities & Investments Commission (ASIC) – The government body that enforces and regulates company and financial services laws to protect consumers, investors and creditors.

Australian Securities Exchange (ASX) – The Australian market for trading shares.

bear market – This occurs when share prices are in a continuing, long-term decline. The worst bear markets can last for many years. There can be market fluctuations up and down within a bear market.

bonds – A fixed-interest debt security issued by a government or a company. The investor who owns the bond receives interest, and the bond is repaid to the investor at the maturity date. Bonds can be traded on the Australian market, which – as with all forms of trading – can result in a profit or a loss. Company bonds can also result in a loss if the company goes out of business before the maturity date.

book value – The net amount shown in a company's accounts for any asset, liability or owners' equity item.

bull market – This occurs when share prices are continually increasing over the long term. Bull markets can last for many years. There can be market fluctuations up and down within a bull market.

capital gain – Growth in the value of an investment.

capital loss – A decline in the value of an investment.

correlation – The degree to which two different investments respond in a similar way to the same circumstances. Shares that are highly correlated respond in a similar way; shares that have low correlation do not.

discounted cash flow (DCF) – Discounted cash flow analysis discounts future free cash flow projections to arrive at a present value. This is then used to evaluate the attractiveness of an investment.

diversification – Spreading investment capital across a range of investments in the hope of limiting the effects of any poorly performing investments.

dividends – A portion of a company's profits that is distributed to shareholders. Usually expressed as an amount of cents per share.

dividend yield – The dividend shown as a percentage of the most recent price for the shares. Helps to assess the rate of return on an investment.

earnings per share (EPS) – The amount of earnings that can be attributed to each share over a 12-month period.

exchange-traded fund – An investment fund that trades on a stock exchange and can be bought and sold like a share.

free cash earnings – Earnings per share less capital and investment expenditure, then add back amortisation and depreciation (non-cash flow items) equals free cash earnings. This can be used to expand the business or pay dividends (or increased dividends) to shareholders.

index fund – A fund that makes a range of investments with the aim of matching a chosen index, and is then listed on the share market.

internal rate of return (IRR) – The rate of return a project can be expected to generate excluding external factors such as changes in interest rates.

intrinsic value – A calculation based on the fundamentals and performance of a business that finds the 'true' value of a share. This is then compared to the current share price to see if the share should be considered for purchase.

margin of safety – Buying assets below their intrinsic value.

market sector – The industry that a company operates in; for example, energy or health care. Companies are grouped according to the Global Industry Classification Standard (GICS).

moving average – An indicator applied to a share price chart that shows the average price of the share over a given period; for example, seven days. It helps to show the trend of the price.

net asset backing – The assets owned by shareholders in a company, expressed as a value per share.

overvalued – A share that is currently selling above its intrinsic value.

price/earnings ratio (P/E ratio) – The number of times the share price covers the earnings per share in a 12-month period.

return on equity – The return a company has provided for the equity invested by shareholders.

robo-advice – The Australian Securities & Investment Commission (ASIC) call Robo-Advice "Digital Advice" because it is undertaken online via computers, tablets, or other smart devices. It adopts algorithms and technology to provide advice in place of a human financial advisor.

share buy backs – A company purchasing its own shares, usually either to increase the value of the shares or reduce the threat of a takeover.

shareholders' equity – The interests of shareholders in the assets of a company.

speculative investment – Buying shares with the aim of making a short-term profit, based on the possibility of a rapid increase in the share price. A high risk, high reward approach.

undervalued – A share that is currently selling below its intrinsic value.

volume – The number of shares that are bought and sold in a given timeframe. Shares that trade in small volumes should be avoided. This is also referred to as 'liquidity'.

CONTACT DETAILS

Mark Wylie
PO Box 63
West Beach South Australia 5024
email: mark.wylie@wylie.com.au

SERVICES INCLUDE

Business advice
Business administration advice
Investment education and books.